When All Was

Well

In Wellwood

Larry Levy

BookLocker
Saint Petersburg, Florida

Copyright © 2020 Larry Levy

ISBN: 978-1-64718-424-7

All rights reserved. No part of this publication may be reproduced, stored in a retrieval system, or transmitted in any form or by any means, electronic, mechanical, recording or otherwise, without the prior written permission of the author.

Published by BookLocker.com, Inc., St. Petersburg, Florida.

Printed on acid-free paper.

The characters and events in this book are fictitious. Any similarity to real persons, living or dead, is coincidental and not intended by the author.

BookLocker.com, Inc.
2020

First Edition

Library of Congress Cataloging in Publication Data
Levy, Larry
When All Was Well In Wellwood by Larry Levy
Library of Congress Control Number: 2020906624

Acknowledgments

There is no greater joy than to write a book about all the things you are grateful for and to acknowledge the wonderful people that made the blessing possible.

I would like to thank my father for, "the roof over my head, the clothes on my back, and the food on our table" and, for so much more.

I would like to thank my mother for her intelligence of heart, love, and generosity in allowing me to become the person I wanted to be.

I would like to thank my brother for all the kicks, the music, the mischief, and the camaraderie through all the twists and turns of childhood and adolescence.

I would like to thank my sister for her spirit and independence and for her part in us becoming the best of friends.

I would like to thank every neighbor, every parent, and every canine that made our neighborhood a place of comfort and fun – a gift that will never be forgotten.

I would like to thank every friend of mine through the early years at Wellwood Elementary and the transitional years at Pikesville Jr. and Sr. High.

And I would like to thank my wife for her love and support even though she grew up in Woodlawn.

And to Angela and Richard Hoy, Ali, Todd Engel, and BookLocker for all their hard work.

This book is dedicated to the memory of Gabe Silber, without whom the neighborhood would have not been the same.

Contents

The Early Years 13

    6707 Chokeberry Road 14
    Burned Beginnings 15
    Hobby Horse Hall 16
    An Early Life in Black and White 17
    A Nice Thing 19
    Wellwood Elementary School 21
    The Pied Piper of Wellwood 23
    Sealtest 24
    Wait a Minute! 25
    A Short Strange Trip 26
    I'm a Believer 27
    Retribution 28
    Wagner's Pharmacy 29
    Baseball Cards 30
    Yeah, Yeah, Yeah 31
    Mickey 32
    First Pitch 33
    Undiagnosed Fear of Clowns 34
    Hopscotch, Anyone? 35
    Greek Dodge 36
    Supermarket Sweep 37
    The Balloon Ascension 38
    Silber's 39
    In the Eyes of the Beholder 40
    The Nehru Jacket 41
    The Chosen People 42
    Romeo and Juliet, Sort of 43
    Our Better Angels 44
    Neighborly Revenge 46
    The Houses of Cool 47
    The Other Half 49
    Cereal Mom 50
    The Whip 51
    The Super Ball 52
    Orange Greed 54

Buck Teeth 55
Wildwood 56

Transitions 57

That and 25 Cents 58
Homesickness 59
Language Skills 60
The Imaginary Line 61
The Baseball Kids and the Shrew 62
Boys Will Be Boys 64
An Incident Involving Birds 66
O, Brother! 67
Nature Abhors a Vacuum Cleaner 68
You're Old Friend, Simon Harris 69
Two Hands Ace 70
The Barber of Pikesville 71
Everything Sounds Better in Stereo 72
Looking Back 74
Thumbs Up 76
Fountain of Youth 78
Thanks, man! 79
Pony Boy 81
Gateway Drug 83
A New Philosophy 84
Baltimore Trick and Novelty 86
The Eldorado Bar 87
The Penny Arcade 88
The Beep Line 89
The Plaza 90
Wallpaper 92
Swimmingly 93
Bombs Away 94
Drum Beats of War 96
Champagne Sparkle 97
The Presence of Soul 98
Ahoy, Landlubbers! 99
The Spring of My Discontent 100
Sunny's 101
As If 102
Spirit in the Sky 103

Almost All the Way 105
The Marriottsville Carnival 106
Mono 108
The Next Level 109
Innocence is Ephemeral 110
Watkins Glen 112
Sweet Cider 114
"It's Aite" 116
My Awakening 118
The Last Day 119

Epilogue 121

You Can Never Go Home 122

It could have been something else,

But it wasn't, it was something great!

The Early Years

Larry Levy

6707 Chokeberry Road

In 1958 my parents bought their first house
After living with my mom's parents
And my dad's completion of his peacetime service in the army.

6707 Chokeberry Road sat comfortably between
Wellwood Elementary School and Pikesville Senior High
In what was referred to as Indian Village.

The houses that lined Chokeberry Road had no trees
A sure sign that suburbanites were moving in.
Each house had a single driveway and one car:
A Chevy, Ford or Dodge usually from the 40's or 50's.

Our split-level, red brick home had three bedrooms upstairs,
A kitchen, dining room, and living room on the first floor,
And unique to our house, both a large recreation and play room,
That occupied two-levels in the basement.

Our neighborhood would have the requisite 2.3 kids,
All conceived around the same time,
Who went to the same schools, played baseball together,
And learned from the values portrayed in "Leave it to Beaver."

Dr. Benjamin Spock instilled confidence in parents everywhere.
He entrusted mothers to follow their instincts
And to be understanding and affectionate with their children.

Yes, all would be well in Wellwood.

Burned Beginnings

The Curtiss-Wright Airport
Used by the flying club of Baltimore
Stood on the south side of Smith Avenue.

The new middle-class residents of Indian Village --
With street names like Cherokee, Chippewa, and Navajo --
Lined up on the north side of Smith Avenue
And watched the old airplane hangar burn to the ground.

Within a year the Greenspring Shopping Center was built
With a drug store and a bowling alley
But no one ever spoke about the airport or the fire.

Larry Levy

Hobby Horse Hall

Every weekday morning a bus stopped at my house
And whisked me away to a farm in rural Maryland.

Hobby Horse Hall was a nursery school
That sat adjacent to the Humane Society
And was more of a camp than a school.

While the other kids in the neighborhood were playing
With building blocks and preparing for kindergarten,
I was learning about dogs, cats, pigs, cows and horses.

It was a strange place to send a young child
Where animals were the primary educational focus.

One day, a sled was hitched to 'Big Red', a usually docile horse.
For some reason Red got spooked
And ran me head first into a wooden fence.

My mother was summoned to attend to my wounds
And my natural refusal to go near any horse again.

That would all change when I was introduced to horse racing.

When All Was Well In Wellwood

An Early Life in Black and White

In 1961 during my fourth year,
I began watching "The Lone Ranger" reruns on television
And became obsessed with the cowboy way of life.

The 'masked man' fought outlaws in the old west,
Bellowed "Hi-ho, Silver! Away!"
From high atop his faithful white horse "Trigger",
And donned cowboy apparel worthy of imitation.

So, my mom bought me my own black and white cowboy suit
That I wore every day --
Around the neighborhood, at family functions,
And when I slept over my grandparent's house.

One day I rode shotgun with my mom
Armed with my plastic, white-handled Colt 45
As we took on the clothing merchants along Reisterstown Road.

After a long day of bartering and fabric rustling
My mom took me for some grub
At Lotus Inn, a Chinese restaurant on the corner of Rogers Avenue.

The wait staff greeted me with the hackneyed "Howdy Partner"
And the "pow-pow" finger gun imitation
As I sat booth-side next to my best gal.

After the meal my mom and I returned home.
When I went into my room, I realized my holster was empty.
I had lost my favorite gun.

Larry Levy

I cried and cried even though I knew cowboys never shed a tear.
But I also knew that a cowboy never went anywhere without a gun.

The next day I decided to hang up my spurs.

A Nice Thing

I went to first grade at Beth Tfiloh
With about twenty other kids who skipped kindergarten.

There were two boys who sat on either side of me;
One with the exact same birthday
And another who was the son of a local celebrity.

The pseudo-famous kid's father
Would come on TV pushing plastic seat covers.
His pitch was, "Get off of that sofa, are you trying to ruin it!"

All the girls in my class
Were drawn to this kid because of his father
Which irritated me to no end.

So, I told my mom
About this pretty girl in my class
That I liked more than any girl in the whole wide world.

My mom suggested bringing the girl a flower.
She cut a single red rose from the side of our house
And told me to give it to my "special friend".

The next day I gave the dark-haired beauty
The red rose from my family's garden.
She smiled and said, "thanks, but I already have a boyfriend."
It was of course, the infamous son-of-the-seat-cover-salesman.

Larry Levy

After recess, I stayed behind when the kids returned to class
Under a weeping willow tree where my broken heart felt at home.
An hour later my teacher realized I was missing and came to fetch me.
She told me, "You did a nice thing."

Wellwood Elementary School

In September of 1963
I began the second grade at Wellwood Elementary
After my one-year stint at Beth Tfiloh.

I was one-year younger than my new classmates
Which a few of the boys gave me a hard time about.
But my chronological deficiency didn't hold me back socially.

Once the kids found out you weren't
A cry-baby, a nose-picker, a paste-eater
Or the most ridiculed of all, a pants-pee-er
You were left alone and accepted into the fold.

On my first day of school,
I was walking past one of the baseball fields
When a few boys I recognized from my class
Pointed and laughed at my crewcut.

We all became friends rather quickly
Once I was able to prove to them
That I was also good at throwing and catching things.

There were a few smart kids and a few dim bulbs
But in general, everyone else was about the same.
It came down to how hard you tried.

And everyone had their own special claim to fame.
Some were excellent at spelling or grammar,
Or able to poll parrot anything they heard or read
While others had a flair for science.

Larry Levy

My early ability was finishing first in the speed math competitions,
Where you folded paper and completed horizontal rows of problems
In addition, subtraction, multiplication and division.

I'm not sure where that got me but I enjoyed the process.
The kids who could burp the alphabet or wiggle their ears,
Were the ones who went on to bigger and better things
Or at least I thought so at the time.

The Pied Piper of Wellwood

Our neighborhood was blessed to have a friendly, fun-loving mailman.
We called him Curly, and like the famous comedian before him,
He loved animals and children.

To the fathers Curly brought bad news:
"Bills, bills, and more bills", my dad would say.
The moms however were charmed by his kindness
Because he adored *their* children.

Curly was the Pied Piper of Wellwood.
He would accumulate kids while walking his route
Telling jokes and acting the clown.

He would hand out candy to his flock
And remembered what each kid's sweet tooth craved.
He used to pump me full of 'Sweet-tarts'
And then go into a rendition of the 'Curly Shuffle'.

He also tore down the barriers between letter carrier and canine
By handing out dog biscuits to the four-legged oppressed.
Somewhere a meeting had taken place where it was decided
Curly was *okay* and could pass in peace.

I never saw a kid cry nor a dog growl in the presence of Curly.
That's how it was back then in Wellwood.

Larry Levy

Sealtest

The kids in the neighborhood used to argue
Over which household had the best milk;
As if the cows had a say in the matter.

There were four local companies serving the Baltimore area –
Sealtest, Cloverland, Greenspring, and Koontz.

Our gunmetal gray milk-box carried the Sealtest logo.
I'm not sure how or why my family came to support Sealtest
But I assumed it was one of those closed-door parental decisions.

I always preferred friends' sleep over my house
Where the milk was a known commodity.
I was way too picky to enjoy cereal with inferior milk.

I would be sitting at the breakfast table
When the milkman would come to our kitchen door.
"Mom, can I have some raisin bread, please, please!" --
The second 'please' always seemed to do the trick.

The milkman would run back to his Sealtest truck
And bring a loaf of warm raisin bread
To a kind mom and a kid waiting with cream cheese and jelly.

Back then a man could earn an honest living
Delivering dairy products and warm bread door to door.
Freshness also came in the form of flirtation
With the rise-and-shine-stay-at-home moms.

Wait a Minute!

The Good Humor Company started in Youngstown, Ohio.
At peak they had some two-thousand ice cream trucks
But kids cared little about such technical facts.

The ubiquitous Good Humor Man --
Fresh out of Good Humor Man School –
Told us jokes and stories about Dixie cups and popsicles,
And shifted our focus from whatever kid-stuff we were doing.

There was the creamsicle, toasted almond, and fudgesicle,
The ice cream sandwich, push-up, and strawberry shortcake,
Along with the famous, thin chocolate over vanilla, on a stick.

My favorite varied from day to day depending on my mood.
I liked everything the Good Humor man was pedaling
Except for the ice cream sandwich.
The chocolate stuck to my fingers and made pitching baseballs a drag.

Two houses up from ours lived a cocker spaniel.
When the sleigh bells rang
From the all too familiar Good Humor truck,
A Dixie cup was placed in her mouth, and off she went.

The three magic words, "Wait a Minute!"
Carried profound significance and were not to be taken lightly.
It meant the difference between a good snack and a bad one.

The universal sugar-craving scream
Was music to the ears of the men in white.

Larry Levy

A Short Strange Trip

At seven years old I was too young to know or care what a bris was
And for obvious reasons could not seem to remember mine.
But my mother thought it necessary for my brother and I
To see my first-cousin go through what was once our fate.

My uncle, the father of the soon to be improved baby boy,
Was in the Air Force and stationed in North Carolina.
My father, happily I suppose, got out of going to the proceedings.

Since neither my brother nor I had any skin in the game, so to speak,
We were looking for something to make the trip worthwhile.
The upside for us came in the form of traveling
From Baltimore to North Carolina by train.

We were not in our seats for more than five minutes
Before the need to explore took over.
While my mother read her fashion magazine,
My brother and I ran from car to car
And from one end of the train to the other.

For lunch we had our first ever ham and cheese sandwich
Which would have made my kosher-keeping grandmother cringe
And anyone hearing about the trip, laugh at the obvious contradiction.

The ceremony was short-lived, a one and done, if you will,
But the festivities continued at the air force base --
The strangest place ever for a sacred religious ritual.

I'm not sure why the removal of a baby's foreskin
Called for a celebration and a fancy deli tray of salted meats,
But I suppose there was a hidden meaning somewhere.

I'm a Believer

My best friend and gal pal in grade school
Had a face full of freckles, wild hair
And the physical strength of a boy.

We caught salamanders in the stream
Played doctor in her den
And cards with her older brother and sister.

During the blizzard of 1966,
While we were digging tunnels in the two-foot snow drifts,
I told her about a new popular song,
"I'm a Believer" which was rocking the airwaves.

Her older sister who looked like Cher
Happened to have a copy of The Monkees' latest album.
After we got out of our wet winter clothes,
My friend and I listened to every track on the record.

When I heard, "I'm a Believer"
I stared straight into her freckled face.
I didn't yet understand the game of love
But I knew somehow, she would be involved.

Larry Levy

Retribution

There was a kid my age who lived across the street.
He used to eat paste and other gross things.
Every neighborhood had one of these kids.
They usually resembled Pugsley Addams.

One day, his father, who resembled Jackie Gleason
And ate many things, gross and otherwise,
Decided to teach his son and I how to box.

A ring was set up in their living room
Which seemed a strange place to rough-house
Considering my parents wouldn't even let me in *their* living room.

So, the dad laced up our gloves
And told us to start punching each other.
I remember getting the best of his son
That angered the dad to no end.

As retribution, their family stole our dog.
Since they had such an abundance of food
They were able to lure our dog away.
I think it was the first known case of dognapping.

When All Was Well In Wellwood

Wagner's Pharmacy

Back in the good 'ole days, pharmacies had lunch counters
With chrome floor mounted bar stools and vinyl red tops
That spun around so you could see the entire store.

While people waited for their prescriptions to be filled
They ordered Stewart sandwiches in plastic bags
That were re-heated in an infrared oven.

My friends and I would ride our bicycles to Wagner's Pharmacy.
We'd sit at the counter, talk and joke with the soda clerk,
Then order coddies with crackers and mustard
And a chocolate soda served in a triangular-tapered paper cup
That sat inside a chrome tulip style holder.

When we were finished eating, we'd buy all the latest in candies:
Waxed lips, Pixie-stix, Lik-m-aid, Turkish taffy, Red Hots,
Fireballs, Jawbreakers, Sweet-tarts, and candy cigarettes.

We bought Spiderman, Superman, and Batman comic books
And Topps baseball cards by the pack – each with a stick of gum.

The ma-and-pa drug store was *the* place to hang
That is, until the pharmacist, and owner of the store
Gave you the, okay-it's-time-for-you-to-go-look.

Then it was back home to appease our youthful addictions.

Larry Levy

Baseball Cards

My love affair with baseball cards began in 1964
When I played for the Cardinals in my first year of little league,
The same year the major league Cardinals won the World Series.

I went through the phase of hanging baseball cards with clothespins
To the spokes of my Huffy bicycle for that motorcycle effect.
But that meant destroying the players I loved.

My brother and I, and two guys from the neighborhood,
Soon realized the value in flipping cards for fun and profit;
Although profit back then was defined as having more cards.

My next-door neighbor had the perfect area for flipping cards;
A long narrow hallway, smooth floor, and doors that could be shut
In case an errant throw ended up as a 'leaner'.

If you had the skill to land your card on top of another card,
You collected the entire lot of cards.
The idea of course was to get rid of your doubles,
And 'flipping' was the best way to get what you didn't have.

Our problem, like many other kids across the country
Was not having the foresight that our favorite players
Easily acquired then would someday be worth a fortune.

And none of our mothers knew either.
To them it was just another toy their kids grew out of
That needed to be thrown away.

In 2010 Topps came out with a series of baseball cards called,
"Cards You Mom Threw Out" to give grown men
Another chance to relive their childhood and forgive their mothers.

Yeah, Yeah, Yeah

In 1964, when the four lovable mop-tops from Liverpool
Brought their, "Yeah, Yeah, Yeah" to the sleepy enclave of Wellwood,
Two entrepreneurial boys with crewcuts came up with a plan.

At ages seven and four respectively,
My brother and I calculated that there was money to be made
Performing Beatles' songs to an unenlightened neighborhood.

Since we were too young to commit to the time and expense
Of playing guitar, bass, or drums
We had to come up with some sort of musical alternative.

Enter the tennis racket.
It looked similar enough to a guitar
And strumming the strings didn't involve
The long hours of practice that a real guitar required.

So, we set out to conquer the world
With our wooden Wilson tennis rackets in hand
And the lyrics to our favorite songs committed to memory.

For a nickel, a family could be serenaded
To, "I Want to Hold Your Hand" or "Please, Please, Me"
Without leaving the comfort of their home.

My brother and I prospered for about a day or two
Until the lack of repeat customers closed the door on our balladeering.
We learned being cute could only get you so far.

Plus, the business changed when The Rolling Stones entered the scene.

Larry Levy

__Mickey__

I was six months into my seventh year when my sister was born.
My mom brought the bundle of joy down into our living room
And laid her down on our purple sofa
Where my dad declared, "wow, she's as brown as a berry."

My sister arrived with her feet hitting the ground
(Having kicked her way out of solitary confinement)
Leaving no doubt that she was a girl on the move.

But every time I saw my sister, she was imprisoned somewhere:
In her high chair, the stroller, or the playpen,
While my brother and I were able to roam freely.

To stave off her obvious resentment,
She took comfort in the form of a white, stuffed animal –
A duck she affectionately called, Mickey.

She took him wherever she went, night and day.
Unfortunately for her internally feathered friend,
He had to be transported by the neck
Which over time caused his head to fall to one side.

My brother and I, being wise guys and tormentors,
Put Mickey in the hall closet when my sister left him unattended.
Then we would slam the door on his already debilitated neck
So, all that was visible was the head of the bulging-eyed duck.

First came the universal cry of, "Maaaaah"
Followed by our laughter and her screams.

Despite my brother and I trying to realign his neck,
Mickey lasted many more years than any real duck would have,
So, no harm, no foul.

First Pitch

When my dad's dream of becoming a baseball player
Was thwarted by the demands of religious parents,
He swore that his kids would circle the diamond
With baseball caps and not yarmulkes.

At age seven he saw in me the ability to throw
So, he worked toward the goal of making me into a pitcher.

His other son, three years my junior,
Was also given the gift of chucking baseballs
By the same creator from whom my father had taken a sabbatical.

My brother was a really, good pitcher.
He was a hard thrower and had pinpoint accuracy.
So, he followed the tradition for all males in our family,
And joined Wellwood Little League as an eight-year old.

On his debut outing, he took the mound
Brimming with confidence and excitement.
As he went into his windup, there was a clap of thunder
And the heavens let loose a torrent of rain.

Everyone, players and spectators alike, ran to their cars
Except my brother who stayed behind, still on the mound.
Eventually, he made his way back to our car
Wet with grief and the fury of the storm.

There were no lightning bolts nor signs of divine intervention
But I'm sure there was anger on both sides of the universe
When my brother's first pitch was not to be.

Larry Levy

Undiagnosed Fear of Clowns

There was a clown from the 60's
That went by the name of Lorenzo who
Appeared every Saturday on WJZ Baltimore.
He was all the rage among the under ten set.

Lorenzo never spoke during his show
But elicited great emotion with his facial movements.
It was serious business being a clown.

The show revolved around Lorenzo's search for a lollipop.
Whenever he found one
He would break into "The Lorenzo Stomp".

All the kids on the set went crazy
When Lorenzo, with his big floppy feet,
Danced to "Yakety Sax".

One Saturday, a bunch of us from the neighborhood
Piled into my friend's father's maroon car
With our tickets to "The Lorenzo Show".

But as my friend's dad started to pull out of the driveway,
I bolted from the back seat and ran home.

No one could figure out why I reacted the way I did.
A team of specialists was sent in
And they concluded I had "Fear of Clowns" syndrome.

Hopscotch, Anyone?

The prettiest girl in our neighborhood
Was well diversified in her attractiveness:
She had a hopscotch court in her driveway.

In order to accommodate the influx of 10-year-olds
Hanging around their home,
Her parents had to park on the street.

There was nothing like standing on one foot,
Hopping and kicking a rubber disk
To test one's endurance and agility.

When she and I weren't listening to Beatles' albums,
We were outside throwing the 'cat's paw'
And trying to run the table from 1 to 10.

Little did I know that my formative years
Would be in training for a hopscotch tournament
Held annually at a day camp I attended one summer.

I entered the tournament as an underdog
And emerged victorious with a trophy full of candy
That I gave away on the bus ride home.

I learned that winning was sweeter than sugar.

Larry Levy

Greek Dodge

In elementary school there was a game known as Greek Dodge,
The origins of which were unknown to us at the time.
All we knew was that we got to throw a ball at someone
Without getting in trouble from a parent or teacher.

The game was played on a tennis court without a net.
Twelve people stood on one side, twelve on the other.
A player ran up to but not over the center line
And hurled a volleyball at someone on the other side.
If the ball was caught, that player was still 'alive'.
But if the ball struck a player,
That player was out until someone caught them back in.
Once all the players on a side were knocked out, the game was over.

The teachers must have called a meeting, probably over drinks,
And decided it was time for the kids who couldn't sit still
To have their day in the sun.

Of course, not every kid was thrilled about playing the game.
A smart chucker could eliminate the easy targets:
Someone picking their nose; two girls talking to each other,
Or a skinny boy bored to tears form a game he was forced to play.

Greek Dodge was a game where the wild ones ruled.

Supermarket Sweep

I was in the fifth grade when word came from on high,
"You can leave school early - your parents are going to be on T.V."

Apparently, my mom and dad had tipped off my teacher
About their contestant status
On a popular show called, "Supermarket Sweep".

The rules were simple:
Wives guessed the price of pre-selected groceries
Which in turn gave the husbands more time
To run around the store with a metal cart and accumulate food.
Victory went to the couple with the highest grocery bill.

One of the contestants was Jim Palmer
Starting pitcher for the Baltimore Orioles.

Neither my parents nor the Palmer's won
But I was the lucky recipient of an autographed baseball
With Palmer's signature, and his backup for the show, Dave McNally.

For months, I kept the baseball in a loving cup in my bedroom.
One day when we went outside for a catch
My friend coerced me into using the autographed ball.
The Spalding horsehide was no match for asphalt and stones.

This was before I understood the value of things.

Larry Levy

The Balloon Ascension

Hands down, one of my favorite events in elementary school
Was the annual spring balloon ascension.

Although none of us could spell the word ascension
Much less use it in a sentence,
We knew a good time when we saw it.

As with all games of chance and competition
There were always rules, arbitrary or otherwise,
And releasing balloons into the upper atmosphere
Came with its own set of requirements.

First came the door-to-door sales approach
Of getting family, neighbors or friends
To support the cause by buying a raffle ticket.

If you were entrepreneurial enough and people cooperated,
You could increase the chances that one of your balloons
Would make its way to California or beyond.

I always had difficulty sleeping the night before the big event
Because I would identify with 'the balloon',
Wondering what the inflated piece of colored rubber
Went through in its journey to the other side of the country.

The horror of seeing one of my new friends stuck in a tree
Was overshadowed by the hope that some pretty girl
In Oshkosh Wisconsin would find my balloon in her front yard,
Write me a letter, and then become one of my best friends.

My teacher told me to take note of my active imagination –
And so, I have.

When All Was Well In Wellwood

Silber's

In the Greenspring Shopping Center, the bowling alley separated
Baskin Robbin's on one side and Silber's Bakery on the other.
By walking no more than twenty-five feet in either direction
Kids could get their sugar fix in frozen or solid form.

Silber's was famous for two things:
Chocolate tops and vanilla cupcakes.
Chocolate tops were a Baltimore original with a very simple design;
Rich, sweet chocolate swirled on top of a vanilla shortbread cookie.

What made Silber's unique however, were their vanilla cupcakes.
The very same chocolate that devilishly sat on top of a cookie
Was also placed on top of a vanilla cupcake
But with a slightly thicker texture.
This allowed the chocolate to be taken off in one piece
So, topping and cake could be devoured separately.

But the little old ladies in hair nets who worked the bakery
Would not just hand over a chocolate top or cupcake.
Each item had to be boxed and tied down with string.

The string came from a large gold canister that hung from the ceiling.
These women were able to tie a box
With the speed and dexterity of a rodeo cowboy.

The father of one of my friends
Owned and managed all the Silber's bakeries.
Sometimes my friend and I would ride our bicycles
Up to the main plant on Reisterstown Road,
Sample the latest in sweets,
And get the freshest cupcakes right out of the oven.

I learned it was always good to have a friend on the inside.

Larry Levy

In the Eyes of the Beholder

In grade school, if I was attracted to a girl,
Or if they began hanging around me more than normal,
I would ask them if they wanted to go steady.

To officially 'go steady'
You had to have an I.D. bracelet
And the bracelet had to be made of gold.

Script lettering was the preferred style at the time.
We had just graduated from block to cursive
So, it showed the girls a degree of sophistication.

If the girl was not taken, she always said "yes"
Which meant a free kiss at some point
And more time holding hands during roller skating.

There was this one girl at Wellwood
Who the boys used to make fun of,
Just because she had a big nose.
I thought she was cute so, I asked her to go steady.

We went to Drug Fair for French fries and a soda,
Talked at night on the phone, smiled at each other in class,
Held hands and kissed after school.

She was the perfect girlfriend for three weeks!

When one of my teachers asked me what,
"Beauty is in the eyes of the beholder" meant,
I told her about the pretty girl with a big nose.

The Nehru Jacket

The Nehru jacket came out in the mid-60's
With a high collar turned up
And a single line of buttons down the center of the coat.

The Indian inspired Nehru was the go-to garb
For up-and-coming British rock stars;
The main impetus for my wanting one.

But my mother wouldn't spring for the expensive garment.
She offered as a compromise, the popular accessories,
The turtleneck and eyebrow raising, medallion.

I opted for a black turtleneck and a silver embroidered medallion
That looked like something a crusader would wear.

I wore my 'getup' every day for months
Until it wasn't cool anymore.

Meanwhile, the Nehru jacket went 'out' as quick as it was 'in'.

Larry Levy

The Chosen People

One of the great coupling ideas
During the elementary school years
Came in the form of indoor roller skating.

For two hours every Saturday and Wednesday after school
All the 5th and 6th graders were invited to the gym
To skate to Three Dog Night or The Foundations
Over the same floor where basketball was played.

The girls lined up on one side of the gym
And the boys on the other.
Like Adam and Eve, one girl and one boy were chosen
To start the process of multiplication.

God was a teacher with a whistle
And by command the first couple would split,
Choose another partner, and so on,
Until every member of the tribe was in motion.

It was all about who chose whom
And the promise of hope to the chosen people.

When All Was Well In Wellwood

Romeo and Juliet, Sort of

When I grew up, everyone I knew had a housekeeper
Who was part of the family,
And doubled as a substitute mom.

We had a rock star for a maid.
She was young, black, and very pretty.
I thought she was one of the Ronettes.

One weekend my parents went away
And she stayed with my brother and I.

I had just drifted off to sleep
When my dog began barking and running in circles
Trying to warn us of some impending doom.
He was a huge Lassie fan so he knew the protocol.

Someone was tossing pebbles at my parent's bedroom window.
That someone was our maid's boyfriend.
He had climbed a ladder and was now staring through the window.
I remember thinking how smart he was for bringing a ladder with him.
Apparently, he had success with this technique before.
But she rebuffed his advances and told him to scram.

I was only twelve years old at the time
And had not read Romeo and Juliet
So, I was not yet knowledgeable in the art of love.

I learned that when pursuing a lover
The woman must have an elevated advantage.
It seemed to work well in high drama.

Larry Levy

Our Better Angels

There was Rocky, Lance, Dolly, Buffy,
Ruby, Muttle, Wally, Peter,
Rags (who my sister liked to call Lad),
And a whole host of other canines
That remained indoors and never sought the spotlight.

But for many families in our neighborhood,
A dog was the four-legged version of another child.
They often acquired cult status, had strong personalities,
And would roam freely throughout Wellwood without fear.

Lance was a collie who chased airplanes in his free time.
Dolly loved ice cream and was a friend to all.
Ruby was shy and standoffish.
Buffy was neurotic and a bit snippy.
Muttle lived in a hall closet and growled when you hung up your coat.
Rags was propagator in chief: for him every day was hump day,
And Wally couldn't be bothered with the canine social scene.

Peter was a black Dachshund
And proof that God had a sense of humor.
Engineered so that nothing underneath
Was chafed when running along concrete,
Pedro, (as he was often called by my neighbor's Spanish maid),
Drank beer from his ceramic bowl and watched football every Sunday.
A hedonist to the very end, Peter was a role model to us all.

And then there was Rocky. Our Rocky. Crazy Rocky.
My sister referred to the half-mad mutt, as "The Wise One".
Hardly an example of self-awareness and calm,
Rocky bit often and bit many, sometimes just for kicks.

When All Was Well In Wellwood

He was never able to overcome the pepper spray
That a petrified mailman shot into his eyes.

Rocky was an outlier in an otherwise peaceful neighborhood,
A rebel without a cause.

Neighborly Revenge

The poodle has the highest intelligence of any breed of dog.
I'm not sure that was the reason
Our next-door neighbor chose to have twelve of them.

My father threw down the gauntlet!
He took our neighbor to court
And forced them to build a fence to reign in
The growing number of free-range poodles.

In celebration of his hard, fought victory
He took my mother out to dinner
Where alcohol was served in abundance.

When he returned home and pulled up in the driveway
He noticed that one of the enemy's curly haired minions
Had crossed the Maginot line.

To his utter amazement
There was a dyed-in-the-wool, hot pink poodle
Sniffing around his yard.

I never saw my father drink again.

When All Was Well In Wellwood

The Houses of Cool

Every neighborhood has one house
That for kids is a sanctuary;
A cool house where all the rules are broken.

I was lucky because my street had two.
My girlfriend at the bottom of Chokeberry Road
Had the only rancher in the neighborhood.

She also had the only carport on the street
With a shed attached to the opposite side of the house
Where we would play hide and seek.

Her parents were divorced and her mom was never home.
This meant we went unsupervised
And could pretty much do whatever we wanted.

The other house was right next-door to mine.
My neighbor was a few years younger than me
But he and I became friends early on.

He had the coolest mom.
She had a big heart on a small frame
And loved all the kids in the neighborhood.

When I slept over his house
We had no bedtime and no rules.
Sometimes, after my parents had been asleep for hours,
She would drive her son and I
To Velleggia's or the Pimlico Hotel for a late-night meal.

Every Sunday during football season, she'd put out a deli tray
And my friend and I along with his dad
Would watch the Colts on a color T.V.

Larry Levy

She bought a beautiful maroon Oldsmobile Toronado
That never ran and remained sidelined in her driveway
A nostalgic reminder of our midnight trips to Little Italy.

The Other Half

Whenever my dad got a hankering for corned beef
He would drive the family down
To the Jewish deli on Lombard Street.

He became very nostalgic when a corned beef called to him;
Took a circuitous route through the worst neighborhoods
Just so he could show us how the other half lived.

He loved the line about "the other half".
He used it whenever my brother or I complained.
It was probably one of his favorite parts of fatherhood.

On one of our trips we drove past a deserted, rundown street.
There were three girls jumping rope
Outside their dilapidated Baltimore rowhome with the marble steps.

It looked like a scene out of the Hitchcock movie, "Marnie".
It was the first time I *really* saw what the other half looked like.

Larry Levy

Cereal Mom

One of the by-products of 60's T.V. shows
Was to 'buy products' advertised during the commercials –
And kids were the perfect dupes.

If breakfast was the most important meal of the day
A bowl full of sugar with a hint of wheat, corn or oats
Was, the ideal way to get kids bouncing off to school.

And my mother, thanks to her easy-going nature,
Made sure we had the largest and most diverse
Selection of cereal anywhere in the universe.

My father kicked off his busy day
With a trough sized bowl of Post Shredded Wheat
Covered in a mound of Domino sugar.

My brother preferred the rush from Kellogg's Frosted Flakes,
While my sister adopted the chocolate twins,
General Mill's Cocoa Puffs and Kellogg's Cocoa Krispies.
My taste for the new and yet to be discovered
Kept me loyal to the variety pack of eight different cereals.

All our friends used to love sleeping over a house
With a three-foot long laminated gray cabinet
Loaded with cereals their moms would never buy.

Always in rotation were: Alpha Bits, Kix, Trix, Wheat Chex,
Rice Krispies, Rice Krinkles, Captain Crunch, Special K,
Sugar Crisp, Total, Raisin Bran, Product 19, and Life.

In our neighborhood and throughout Wellwood
There was no parallel to our Cereal Mom.

The Whip

During the summer months
Our neighborhood was serviced and entertained
By roving entrepreneurs.

The favorite for us kids was The Whip --
A giant truck with an outer steel mesh cage
And individual saucers that went around on an oval track.

The guy who owned and operated The Whip was a guy named Ed.
He would make the cups go faster the more we screamed.
Somewhere he learned that centrifugal force made kids happy.

One day Ed and his amusement ride on wheels, stopped coming.
I asked my dad if he knew why.
All he said was, "you can't make a living by having fun."

Larry Levy

The Super Ball

One of the greatest inventions during my childhood
Came in the form of a hard piece of circular rubber
That had more movement than a thousand davening rabbis.

The Superball was the ADD of balls.
It bounced higher than a tennis ball,
Could go farther than a Wiffleball or Pinky,
And was not as hard as a baseball or golf ball.

Naturally, it was not enough to try and control the ball
As you would when dribbling a basketball, No!
We, meaning my brother and I,
Had to see how far we could push the limits of bounce.

We would throw it against our bedroom wall
Then watch it break something as it whizzed by our heads.
When our parents reiterated their cries of, "outside!",
We would hit the ball with a bat or chuck it as far as we could
Only to see the small black orb disappear into the woods.

One day my mother took us food shopping at the A&P.
As she was minding her own business pushing the shopping cart,
My brother and I entertained a different idea about nourishment.

In the front of the store was one of those metal, display trees
With the white, extended arms holding bags and bags of Superballs.
So, he and I decided to tear open the bottom of every bag,
Then watch hundreds of Superballs bounce their way to freedom.

My brother and I bolted from the store.
Looking back, we saw the manager yelling at my mother.
We knew that when pointing took place,
Punishment was not far behind.

It was the first time we had ball privileges taken away from us.

Orange Greed

My father used to say of my grandfather (his father-in-law)
"He's the kind of guy who squeezes the juice
From an orange, then throws away the orange."
My grandfather was a capitalist.

My grandmother, the capitalist's wife,
Showed me how to suck the juice from an orange
Using "The World's Smallest Juice Extractor" --
A plastic 'screw-gee' that tapped the skin for liquid gold.

My mother, their daughter, gave me what I really wanted --
Donald Duck orange juice every morning without limits.
I was sure the color of my pee was from drinking so much juice.

Me, the descendent of "10 Things to Do with Oranges"
Found love from the claws of a Coca Cola machine.

I gave my first sip of Fanta orange soda
To a pretty girl at an arts and crafts summer camp.
She finished half the bottle then wiped the orange
On her sleeve in one deliciously greedy motion.

Buck Teeth

Hyperbole is to truth
As an overbite is to a perfect set of teeth.
And what I had was a perfect pair of buck teeth.

My mouth looked like one of those characterizations
Of a man imitating a giant rabbit
Where the two front teeth stuck out past the top lip.

I used to fantasize in my mind –
(the part not blocked by my oversized choppers) –
About a western hero named Buck Teeth.

Buck would ride into town on a dappled grey horse.
He was dressed in a cowboy outfit of black and white
Like I wore every day when I was five years old.

He would seek revenge on all the bullies
And put all the highfalutin girls in their place.
Plus, he could clean an ear of corn like nobody's business.

But one day Buck was gun downed
By an orthodontist who found it necessary
To straighten 'ole Buck out.

And said the orthodontist,
"Good riddance to Buck Teeth and his protruding ways."
I was saddled with braces for the next two years.

Wildwood

It was like a magical kingdom beyond the horizon.
Very few people in Baltimore had ever heard of Wildwood
But my parents had done their research.

My father had to work the weekend of our debut journey
So, he employed my godmother, who brought her eldest son,
And asked her father to supply the wheels.

The car in question was a late 50's Cadillac with fins
That sailed down I-95 to our destination.

Wildwood Crest, New Jersey was an up-and-coming resort.
With its heavy doo-wop and mid-century influence
It was the neon jewel on the eastern seaboard.

We stayed at the Eden Roc,
An L-shaped motel with an aqua neon logo.
It had a small luncheonette, a room air conditioner, and a pool.

The T.V. show, "I Dream of Jeannie" began in 1965.
For the next several years when we returned to the Eden Roc
I kept waiting for Barbara Eden to appear.

Transitions

That and 25 Cents

In 1968, when Baltimore erupted in flames
My father didn't understand the whys and wherefores:
He owned a pharmacy safely tucked away in the suburbs.

Sometimes, I felt sorry for my dad
When he had to make good on his parenting skills
And explain why bad things happened.

That year was the first time I had felt depressed
Even though I had no idea what the term meant.
The generally accepted explanation for my condition
Was the arrival of puberty.

I knew something was up when my dad said, "I want to talk to you".
I figured he had had a closed-door session with my mother.
He told me he was as happy as a lark
Until he turned twenty-eight and starting feeling sad for no reason.
I thought it had something to do with not trusting anyone over thirty.

I once said to my father in a moment of philosophical fervor.
"Experience is the greatest tool, and a fool can learn by no other."

My father responded in his usual witty and cavalier way;
"That and 25 cents will get you a cup of coffee".

Homesickness

When I was twelve years old
I went away to sleep over camp
But hated being separated from the action at home.

Camp Airy was a popular destination
For kids wanting to get away from their parents
And for parents wanting to get away from their kids.

Every morning at 7 a.m.,
The P.A. system blasted songs from the musical, "Hair";
A wake-up call for a brand, new day.

But I pined for my friends back home.
I knew they were playing baseball and basketball without me.
Wondering what the girls in the neighborhood were up to
Made me miss being home more than anything else.

Camp Louise, our sister camp, held bi-monthly dances
That provided some relief from the pangs of homesickness.

Even though the excitement of a new girl was of great comfort,
My father's words echoed in my mind,
"Never give up an old friend for a new one."

Larry Levy

Language Skills

In late August of my twelfth year,
During the annual family pilgrimage to Wildwood,
I ventured into the ocean to body surf.

To my immediate left and all alone,
Was the prettiest girl I had ever seen
Swimming alone, bobbing in and out of the breakers.

When our eyes met, she smiled, and then quickly looked away.
I said something to her about how rough the waves were,
To which she replied, *"Oui, ils sont"*,
That sounded like something I had heard in a "Pepe Le Pew" cartoon.

So, it was time to consult the expert in love.
I swam to shore and told my father of the meeting
And asked his advice on how to proceed.

He quickly determined the language to be French
And had me memorize my opening line,
Voudriez-vous marcher avec moi? --
(Would you like to take a walk with me?)

My new paramour and I took a walk along the water,
Held hands, and spoke the language of puppy love.
When it was time for her to leave and go back home to Quebec
She gave me her address and a kiss on the cheek.

But perhaps the happiest person of all
Was my dad, who got to use his language skills
In a practical manner that he could never have imagined.

The Imaginary Line

When the group of neighborhood pre-teens
Got bored sitting around talking on a side porch,
We sought relief in what kids do best – run.

Capture the flag always took place on a summer night
In the backyards turned in on themselves
That provided the perfect landscape for running.

Teams were chosen and an imaginary line drawn.
The purpose of the game was to take the flag
From the opposition's tree and return unscathed to your side.
But if you were touched while in enemy territory,
It was off to jail until someone from your side set you free.

The line that separated the two sides went on to infinity
Which meant it was legal to go home for awhile
Or cross Smith Avenue, run around Wellwood Elementary,
And emerge from the darkness on the enemy side.

One night I crossed the imaginary line that went on forever
On the back side of Wellwood in the very classrooms
Where I learned about other imaginary lines,
The equator, the prime meridian, and the international date line.

I sat down on my side of the line, in the safe zone,
Far away from the game, the flags, and the neighborhood kids.
I thought about the meaning of infinity, how far I could go,
And that if everyone else was as immobilized as I was
The game would go on forever or become meaningless.

This was the first time I remember being weighed down by abstractions.

Larry Levy

The Baseball Kids and the Shrew

Playing baseball with a tennis ball
Gave us neighborhood kids a practical
And safe way to do what we loved
Without the possibility of breaking any windows.

The desired place was at the appliance dealer's house
On the corner of Chokeberry and Darwood Drive.
The backyard was flat, void of trees,
And large enough to make the game fun.

We played three-on-three or four-on-four
With an automatic pitcher and catcher,
One or two infielders, and an outfielder.

The owner was cool and left us alone
Despite the fact we destroyed his lawn
And hit so many line drives at his rainspout
That it hung on and wobbled like a bad tooth.

Our only problem was their next-door neighbor.
The houses were separated by a small hill,
Barely enough to stop the passed balls by the catcher.

This of course meant we had to trample
On the lawn of a crotchety old woman
And retrieve the ball from the bushes.

Without fail, every time we played a game,
The woman would scream at us, and have her son
Come out of the house and take our game ball.

When All Was Well In Wellwood

Sometimes we didn't even wait for Halloween
To seek our revenge and drive the old biddy
Even more mental, if that was possible.

We'd break a stink bomb inside her Baltimore Sun
Then place the newspaper up against her front door
And let the liquid sulfur do its job.

On one special occasion,
One of the older guys, and a sure-handed shortstop,
Emptied bags of bush and shrub clippings all over their lawn.

I devised a plan where a large rock was tied
And taped to the window unit air conditioner
Just outside their living room.

I stayed out of sight and secured the rock in such a way
That when the rope was pulled,
It would hit against the metal, and to paraphrase Dylan,
"Shook their windows and rattled their walls."

This would cause one of the family members
To come outside and inspect the premises and then retreat.
After a few minutes, I'd start the process all over again.

But none of these clever actions ceased the state of war
That existed between us baseball kids,
And the shrew who ruined our good time.

In the end, we gave up the fight
When we moved on to other more interesting adventures,
Namely girls, and everything that entails.

Larry Levy

Boys Will Be Boys

In a neighborhood where boys threw anything not tied down,
The peach and the apple were at the top of the projectile chain.

We tested our accuracy by trying to hit stationary objects;
Stop signs, telephone poles and lampposts.
When that became boring, we progressed to moving cars and buses
Which proved more challenging because you had to 'lead' the object.

When all else failed we turned to throwing things at each other.
This inevitably resulted in a battle that lasted for hours.

World War III began on a Spring day in 1969.
We represented 'The North', had the best pitching arms,
And the advantage of a fenced-in-yard with a peach tree.
But 'The South' outnumbered us four to one.

The enemy had sent a spy by bicycle
To see if we were vulnerable on our eastern flank.
In response, I let fly an apple fresh from the refrigerator
At the pesky snoop who had infiltrated our ranks.
But it was the second apple that separated boy from bicycle.

Meanwhile, my brother had concocted a brilliant strategy.
The Southern girls had set up a hospital on the porch
On the other side of my neighbor's yard.
My brother began lofting peaches in their direction.
Seconds later came the cries from a Southern nurse.
The fighting immediately ceased and everybody took off.

The father of the wounded girl came running out of his house
Looking for answers and seeking justice.

When All Was Well In Wellwood

My neighbor's dad, inspecting the damage to his house,
Headed him off at the pass and replied to the angry father,
"What's the big deal, boys will be boys!"

Larry Levy

An Incident Involving Birds

One day I walked into my parent's bedroom.
It was Saturday, and my allowance was past due.

My dad was standing at the side window in his underwear.
He was shooting at birds on a telephone wire
With the BB gun he bought me
After I promised to improve my posture.

He claimed the birds woke him up too early
Although no one else was affected by their trilling.

My mother was lying on the bed
Reading Good Housekeeping Magazine.
Back then wives took an interest in their husband's hobbies.

My dad was living out the Groucho Marx joke
About shooting an elephant in his pajamas.
Our family had a good sense of humor.

Years later when I met my future wife
She recalled her father shooting birds
For crapping on his car.
But he wore pants.

O, Brother!

The tradition of handing down the lawnmower
From father to son was probably the result
Of dads everywhere wanting cheap labor.

The only Briggs and Stratton engine I wanted to see
Was on a mini bike or go cart
Not on a machine designed to take my free time away.

Once a week, from Spring to Fall,
It was my job to keep our lawn
As manicured as a golf course.

A friend of mine anchored with the same responsibility
Suggested I run with the mower
To complete the onerous task as quick as possible.

My father put the kibosh on my new technique
Citing the obvious discrepancies in the length of his grass.

So, I did what oldest sons do –
I turned the job over to my younger brother.

Larry Levy

Nature Abhors a Vacuum Cleaner

I despised raking leaves.
"Let them eat Mulch,"
I said to grass and father alike –
Father who held over me the threat of no allowance.

Bamboo shoots blew down on us
From our next-door neighbor's overgrown Zen garden
That was the bane of my father's existence.

I was certain my dad spent his quiet hours
Reading fantasy books like "The Hills Are Alive Sans Leaves"
Or, "How to Get Your Child Interested in Raking"
That gave examples of kids who refused to do yard work.

His worship of grass was quite different
From the hippie's love of the green stuff
I had been reading about with newfound interest.

What mattered most to me and my simple way of thinking
Was how to get out of something I didn't want to do.
The removal of the fallen from God's lazy earth
Was not my idea of fun.

Like Sisyphus, it was an exercise in futility --
Trying to stop running bamboo
That doubled in size every year.

Note to self: Never use a Hoover to do a rake's job.

When All Was Well In Wellwood

You're Old Friend, Simon Harris

One of the great joys of being an athletic youth in the 60's and 70's
Was shopping for sporting goods at Simon Harris.
They dealt in seconds and merchandise rejected for various reasons.

Located on 220 North Gay Street under the Jones Falls Expressway
Just south of the creepy Baltimore City Penitentiary,
Simon Harris was the place to go for bargain hunters.

I bought a baseball glove for seven dollars
Because the Wilson logo was sewn on backwards.
It became my go-to glove for my entire little league career.

My most expensive but favorite purchase of $17.50
Was for a beautiful pair of leather Converse All-Stars
With a minor blemish on the back of the shoe.

I remember rummaging through a box of t-shirts
With logos from colleges no one ever heard of.
For 50 cents you had yourself a one-of-a-kind relic.

A friend up the street had a backyard basketball court
Where we played '21' and '2-on-2' for years.
Whenever he took a shot from beyond the foul line he would say,
"The kid from Idaho State hits one from the outside."

He always wore his Idaho State t-shirt from Simon Harris with pride.

Larry Levy

Two Hands Ace

While I was being prepped for the big leagues
My dad would throw me grounders and pop-ups
To make sure I understood baseball was not all about hitting.

One of the first rules about catching fly balls
Was to make sure you covered the glove
With your free hand after making the catch.

Like most kids who became adept at catching
I got in the lazy habit of using only my glove hand
That prompted my dad's sonorous refrain, "two hands ace".

In high school, I sat in on a typing class
To avoid taking more serious subjects like science.
When I refused to type with both hands
I found myself in biology dissecting starfish.

I had a friend who flunked his driving test
Because he would not comply with the 10 and 2 hand position.
He drove with his right hand at 12 o'clock
And for some reason always got the girl,
Negating the moral of this story.

The Barber of Pikesville

He was a man like any other man
Only his trade was trimming and cutting
"The part of the face above the eyebrows."

His name was Frank
And when it came to cutting hair
He was as frank as Frank could be.

He specialized in stories
About his coming of age
When men with short hair ruled the earth.

Frank thrived during the Vitalis and Brylcreem age
When parents still controlled the length of their children's hair.

In a magical place called Pikesville
There was a direct correlation
Between a young boy's freshly mowed whiffle cut
And the manicured grass of a suburban front yard.

Frank tried to make a go of it
Acquiescing to the new dry look and longer sideburns
But he retired his shears when the hippies came to town.

Larry Levy

Everything Sounds Better in Stereo

When my grandparents traveled to Japan in the early 70's,
My grandfather bought all kinds of stereo equipment
And had it shipped back to his house.

It was very exciting watching him unpack all the boxes
And witness the latest and greatest in the audio world
Just like my brother and I read about in Stereo Review magazine.

He bought a Sansui AM/FM receiver,
A gorgeous Dual 1219 automatic turntable in a wood base,
And two of the ever popular Dynaco A-25 speakers.
Unique to his system, was a Teac reel to reel player/recorder.

Around this time, Gordon Miller Music in Pikesville
Which sold musical instruments and offered lessons,
Sectioned off a part of their store for the sale of stereo equipment.

My brother and I would take every opportunity
To frequent the store and check out the new audio gear.
Not to be outdone by my grandfather's grandiose style,
We had to come up with a way of acquiring quality pieces.

So, we made deals with 'Dave', a fast and friendly salesman of,
Marantz, Sansui, Pioneer, Dual, Garrard,
Dynaco, Wharfedale, AR, and KLH, to name a few.

For a small, initial investment, we were able to barter our way
Up the chain from mediocre to fine equipment
While training our ears and educating our minds
About acoustics and how best to rock the house.

When All Was Well In Wellwood

Our hobby, initiated and encouraged by my grandfather,
Taught us about quality, value, and how to buy, sell and trade.
Of course, the most important thing of all was
How to make our Beatles and Stones records sound the best.

Larry Levy

Looking Back

My grandparents, on my mother's side,
Lived on Old Court Road about ten minutes from our house.
During the summer months we were there almost every day.

The four-acre property had a stone and wood rancher,
A separate building that housed a garage, an office for my grandfather,
And a changing room with a shower.

Heaven was just outside a sliding glass door
That led to a 50' x 25' in-ground swimming pool.
Our family took full advantage of *Shangri La* whenever we could.

My mother was partial to sunbathing and hanging in the shallow end.
My father, who never learned how to dive,
Held his nose and jumped into the deep end.
My brother and I raced or threw things at each other,
And my sister, the fish, swam faster than us all.

Sometimes during the week, my mother dropped me off
To hang out with my grandparents, eat lunch, and swim.
It was a completely different experience playing in the pool alone.

My grandfather, certainly no fan of rock 'n roll,
Blasted WCAO or WKTK through a green, metal, mono speaker
That hung on the underside of the roof and faced the pool.

On one special occasion I heard Scott McKenzie sing,
"San Francisco (Be Sure to Wear Flowers in Your Hair)",
As I bobbed in and out of the water.

When All Was Well In Wellwood

I fantasized about San Francisco, the hippies, the beautiful girls,
The music, peace and love, and "people in motion".
It was the first time I felt my spirit leave my body –
The first time I went somewhere without physically going anywhere.

Looking back, the confluence of song and water took me where I needed to go.

Larry Levy

Thumbs Up

When the parental taxi service was unavailable
And we couldn't carry packages on our bicycles,
My friends and I took matters into our own hands,
Stuck out our thumbs, and hitchhiked to wherever we needed to go.

Hitchhiking was an accepted mode of transportation
Given our pre-sixteen status and the fact
That bad things didn't happen in early 70's suburbia.

One Saturday after several failed attempts to get home
My friend and I became frustrated.
A young guy driving a green Mustang looked at us,
Started to slow down, but changed his mind and kept going.

My friend dropped his thumb
And lifted his middle finger in the direction of the Mustang.
The guy slammed on his brakes, threw the car into reverse,
And came to a screeching halt right where we were standing.

He leaned over, opened the passenger door, and said, "Get In!"
My friend and I looked at each other, nodded, and got in the back seat.
"Where are you going?", he asked, in a really, creepy voice,
To which I replied, "Sanzo and Smith, sir".

He closed the door after us and started driving,
Then looked in the rearview mirror and said,
"You know, I don't appreciate you giving me the finger."

The guy dropped us off at the corner of Sanzo and Smith
And said to us after we were safely out of his car,
"You kids shouldn't hitchhike; it could be dangerous."

When All Was Well In Wellwood

My friend and I split up and went home for dinner.
Next weekend we were back on Sanzo with our thumbs up.

Larry Levy

Fountain of Youth

My uncle, on my mother's side of the family
Made a fortune in the tooth business
And bought himself a brand new, 1970 yellow Corvette.

His job was to drive me to my grandparent's house
For a luncheon and the obligatory cheek pinching
After I had read from the Torah and become a man.

My religious transformation was as quick
As going from 0-60 mph in under 5 seconds.

We were the first to arrive at the party
And my uncle was the first to leave.

While I was being showered with gifts and wisdom
My uncle was shifting gears on the backroads
And becoming a boy once again.

Thanks, man!

The party after a Bar Mitzvah had less to do
With a boy becoming a man in a religious sense
And more to do with a boy becoming a man
By asking a girl out on a date.

There was a tradition, a tacitly accepted agreement
Between the newly crowned thirteen-year-old males,
That when your special day came up on the social roulette wheel
You had first dibs at any girl in the entire grade.

If I really wanted to have a great time with someone super nice
I'd ask this good friend of mine who lived in Chokeberry Court.
She was smart, easy to talk to, and I had known her since 5th grade
When her family moved to Wellwood from Florida.

But after months of consideration,
I chose a classmate of mine who lived outside of Wellwood
Because I didn't think anyone would ask her to my party.

My father doubled as chauffer and part-time chaperone
Which gave him the authority to advise me
On how to treat a girl like a lady.

This involved being well-groomed: hair, suit and tie;
Addressing my date's parents as 'Sir and 'Ma'am',
And opening the car door and letting my date in first.
After the party, it meant walking my date up to her front door
Before any kissing took place.

During the party there was no fatherly advice,
Although I made sure I danced every slow dance
With the girl I came with.

Larry Levy

The morning of a Bar Mitzvah was all about becoming a man
But the evening celebration was all about becoming a gentleman.

Pony Boy

In 1970, after graduating from Wellwood Little League,
I continued my baseball career at Northwest Pony's;
The next rung in the ladder for those serious about the game.

I went from forty-five-feet to sixty-feet, six-inches,
Had to run ninety-feet from base to base,
And wear metal spikes in the process.

In my first outing, I pitched a complete 7-inning game,
And fanned thirteen batters as our team went on to win 1-0.
I completed my first season with a 4-3 record
And a whole new set of friends.

The next year the league moved its location
To Pimlico Junior High School --
Another city field with a professional sized diamond.

One day when I wasn't on the mound,
My coach put me at third base.
A throw came in from the outfield
And the runner unintentionally slid into me with his spikes up.

He shredded my pants from knee to knee
And I had to leave the game and go to the emergency room.
With seven stitches and a three-inch gash on my upper right thigh,
I escaped singing soprano by 'a hair'.

The next day I went to school, limping and lucky,
With a crutch tucked underneath my arm.

Larry Levy

This cute girl in my Spanish class with whom I had struck out before,
Showed sympathy for my injury,
And gave me another chance at bat.

I learned something new about another game I loved.

When All Was Well In Wellwood

Gateway Drug

My best friend and I would go to Woolworths
And for 29 cents buy those little green turtles
That clutched and clawed by the hundreds in a large plastic tub.

Our first inclination was to treat them as pets.
We gave them names like, "Mr. Green Jeans", and "Joey Short Legs"
But they only lived about one week.

So, realizing that attachment was impossible
We turned names into numbers
And began racing them every Saturday in my basement.

We made a few bucks but the thrill was short lived
Because most of the turtles never came out of their shells
And the same turtle kept winning every race.

We moved on to playing poker
After school with some of the neighborhood guys
But my friend and I lost as much as we won.

Another schoolmate of ours who lived a few streets behind me
Was a real wise guy with a great sense of humor.

He would join the weekly card game
And when it was time to buy in on chips
He would pull out a single quarter from his pants pocket.

My friend and I grew agitated knowing
The most we could win from this guy was 25 cents.
So, we decided it was time for a new fix,
Something that could make us some real money.

Larry Levy

A New Philosophy

One Saturday in the Spring of 1970
Toward the end of eighth grade,
My best friend's dad took his son and I to Pimlico Race Course.

He taught us how to read a racing form,
The ins and outs of past performances,
And how to analyze the speed ratings.

Then he showed us the paddock
Where we could check out the horses before each race
And watch the jockeys take their mount.

As he narrowed down his choices for the upcoming race,
He stopped and glanced at the current odds on the tote board
And took us up to the betting window
Where we eagerly watched his every move.

He ended up winning about $20 on the day
Filling both our impressionable young minds with hope
And the promise of a quick return.

Now that betting was 'parent approved'
My friend and I took the gamble
Of cutting school and taking the bus to the track.

One morning we each feigned sickness,
Waited for our parents to leave for the day
And then met up to catch the #5 bus.

We each took our weekly allowance of $10
And hid behind the Baltimore Hebrew sign on Park Heights Avenue
So that no one could see us waiting for a city bus on a school day.

When All Was Well In Wellwood

We came home that day with empty pockets,
And a new philosophy of rationalization,
"You can't put a price tag on having a good time."

Larry Levy

Baltimore Trick and Novelty

The #5 bus turned around at Park Heights and Slade,
Went past Pimlico Race Course and Mondawmin Mall,
Then dropped my friends and I off at the Bromo Seltzer Tower.

We had discovered, via the Yellow Pages,
The answer to every wise-guy kid's dream –
Baltimore Trick and Novelty.

Our fathers worked hard to keep us in middle-class comfort.
But there was something oddly intriguing
About peddling fake vomit and stink bombs for a living.

I remember spending my entire allowance
On a present for my dad that I bought at the novelty store.
The gift was a decorative box with a picture of a suave Frenchman
And the words, "French Birth Control" on the outside.
His birthday surprise was opening the box
To find a miniature guillotine inside.

He had never dealt with visual punchlines before
Nor had a son who reinvested *his* money
In such a non-practical manner.

I think my father and I reached a new level
Of understanding that day.

The Eldorado Bar

Two doors down from Baltimore Trick and Novelty –
On our way to Nedick's for some French fries –
My friend and I passed The Eldorado Bar.

The recessed entrance to the club had an exposed window
Just high enough to stand on tiptoes
And catch a glimpse of the goings on inside.

There was a scantily clad woman sitting on an older man's lap.
The only time I had ever seen such an occurrence
Was over my grandparent's house at a large family gathering
When my grandmother sat on my grandfather's lap.
But my grandfather never smiled like this guy.

When the festivities subsided
The woman looked up and caught my eye.
She smiled and motioned for me to come inside the bar.
My friend and I bolted, laughing as we ran.

But I'll never forget the smile and that look –
A look I would come to understand years later.

Larry Levy

The Penny Arcade

After we left Nedick's and turned left back on to Baltimore Street,
We continued our adventure at the Penny Arcade
Where in fact every game was a nickel.

Neither my friend nor I were particularly good at pinball
But there was something exciting about the lights and noise
Generated from so many machines played by so many kids.

The arcade had every current pinball machine, flippers and all,
And we always left the place more stimulated than when we came in;
Good for my friend and I but aggravation hours later for our parents.

One Saturday afternoon while my friend was playing "Hot Rods",
I finished out my game of "Grand Slam" and went to get more nickels
From the change booth at the front of the store.

When I came back to check on my friend
A kid a few years older than me and a few inches taller
Pulled out a penknife and pushed it up against my stomach.
He said, "give me a dollar or I'll stick ya."

I gave him the dollar and he and his accomplice took off laughing.
I told my friend what had happened but we both shrugged it off.

This type of thing never happened in Wellwood.

The Beep Line

Back when rotary dial phones ruled,
There was a telecommunication loophole
Known as the 'Beep Line'.

411 was the universal number for information
But 211 and 311 produced a siren song
For teenage boys and girls anxious to meet someone new.

The space between the phone-off-the-hook alarm
Was the time to make your presence known,
"Is there anyone out there?"

I was successful on my very first try.
I set up a date for a Saturday after a Friday night marathon.

It was the first time
I arranged my social life
By filling in the blanks.

Larry Levy

The Plaza

The Reisterstown Road Plaza or
'The Plaza' as it was affectionately known,
Opened as an outdoor mall back in 1962,
And became the go-to place to shop in Northwest Baltimore.

My first experience at the Plaza, as a toddler back in the early 60's,
Was at Hess Shoes that also doubled as a barber shop.
I watched electric trains go around
On a track suspended from the ceiling,
While getting a fashionable crewcut and a pair of Jack Purcell's.

I bought my first little-man suit at Hamburgers,
Then "ran right to Reads" and ate at their lunch counter.
If my mom made an entire afternoon out of shopping,
We picked up all our groceries at Food Fair before heading home.

When I got a little older, around eleven or twelve,
My friends and I would hitchhike up to the Plaza
To buy albums at Hecht Company or Stewarts.

There were two stores that punctuated
My transition into the teen years;
Hong Kong which sold posters, blacklights, and paraphernalia, and,
Pennyback which was my first exposure to hippie clothing.

On Saturdays, after a Friday night of beep-line frenzy,
My best friend and I would meet girls outside of the theatre.
If they followed through on their promises, we'd catch a movie,
And then a burger and fries at Hot Shoppes Jr.

One Saturday I rode my Schwinn 10-spd up to the Plaza,
Parked in the bike rack in front of the Pretzel stand,
And went in to my new favorite record store, For the Record.

When All Was Well In Wellwood

When I came back, my bike was gone.
The woman operating the pretzel stand
Turned her eyes away when I looked at her for help.
I knew she knew who it was that stole my bicycle.

I was upset at the woman's silence and the wrong that had been done.
The injustice of it all depressed me more than losing my bike.
My father however, explained things in financial terms.

Larry Levy

Wallpaper

One day my mother made an executive decision
To redecorate my bedroom
In a manner appropriate for a teenager.

As a champion of her eldest son's creativity
She handed aesthetic control over to me
With the understanding that I would "choose wisely".

We went to several wallpaper stores
And pored over hundreds of swatches.

I decided on a mod blue, green, and white design
That pulsated with the slightest movement of your head
Like the logo for the television series, "The Green Hornet".

Naturally, I wanted *all* four walls covered –
A visual manifestation
Of the psychedelic music that swirled in my head.

My father, the wallpaper-hanger-in-chief
Emphatically stated, "No way! –
That crazy pattern will keep you up all night!"

So, a compromise was reached –
One wall and a trash can
Where I discarded any ideas of rebellion.

Swimmingly

When you are in your early teens, the things we do for love
Could be better stated as, the things we do for the mysterious
Attraction we don't yet know anything about.

Such was the case the first time I entered,
The Sunshine Waterbed Company, a small boutique
Located in the basement of a building off Reisterstown Road.

All it took was one visit to the store
And the allure of a slightly older, tall, lithe, blond salesgirl
To win me over, easily convince my accommodating mother,
And appeal to my father's more prurient understanding
Of how life worked.

For $99 of my own money that I had saved for something 'cool',
I got the waterbed, the inner liner, and the wood frame.

But 'Sunshine' also sold sheets, pillows, candles, and incense,
That, of course, meant more trips to the store,
And more time hanging around this girl who took me
From a dull, rigid, mattress and box spring
To an oceanic experience one foot from the floor.

With images of hippie girls from Woodstock and Monterey
I found a new muse to lull me swimmingly to sleep.

Larry Levy

Bombs Away

By the time high school rolls around,
You have acquired enough smarts
To come up with clever and outlandish ideas,
And just enough stupidity to carry them out.

There was a boy in our school, brilliant in science,
Who sold my best friend and I a Dixie cup full of gunpowder,
Showed us how to roll our own casings,
And turned us on to a book called, "Pyrotechnics".

The first test site was outside the backdoor at my friend's house.
We put an M-80 in a miniature metal Fort Knox safe
That was completely flattened and sent sailing over the roof.
My friend's mom was standing at the back door
When the explosion took place waiting to dole out punishment.

The next test took place at my house where we built a Roman Candle.
The device failed to launch after several attempts
And burned a large red circle into my father's prized backyard grass.
I was grounded for a week, not unlike the firework that went nowhere.

My friend and I were making M-80's at a faster rate
And setting them off all over the place:
At the high school, under the bleachers, and in neighbor's trash cans.

We decided that I should store them at my house
So, I put about twenty-five in a brown-paper bag
And kept them under my bed.

One night I was lying awake unable to sleep.
I was worried the fireworks were too close to the heating vent
And going to simultaneously explode,
Sending me into orbit as my house burned to the ground.

The next day I threw all the M80's away
And gave up all aspirations of becoming a pyrotechnician.

Larry Levy

__Drum Beats of War__

There were a few guys in and around Wellwood
That played orchestral instruments in grade school
And took the leap into the world of rock 'n roll.

A friend who lived a few streets over on Laurelwood Drive,
Played bass clarinet and switched over to electric guitar.
He bought a Fender Jaguar and a Sunn Amplifier.

He was a great player and very creative.
I used to go over his house, hang out in his bedroom,
Sit in a beanbag chair, and listen to Black Sabbath.

Another friend that lived on Maurleen Road,
Played saxophone and changed to electric bass.
We spent many hours listening to Steppenwolf records.

Then there was a guy in band class who played the snare drum.
We played baseball together in Northwest pony league
And quickly became friends.

He had a beautiful 5-piece Ludwig silver sparkle drum set.
When I saw him play "Aqualung" by Jethro Tull
I knew that the drums were for me.

So, thanks to an intervention from my mother
Who somehow convinced my father,
I was finally able to play a relevant instrument.

That is when the drum beats of war began.

Champagne Sparkle

The year was 1972, and the place was Timonium.
My mom drove me and $300 to the house
Of a guy who was selling a set of 1964 Ludwig drums.

It was a 4-piece set: bass drum, snare, rack tom and floor tom,
In champagne sparkle which was also called 'pink champagne'.
Included were Zildjian cymbals all around,
And the necessary hardware; stands, pedals, and a throne.

The very first week I began to jam with a friend,
Another fine guitar player who used be a trumpet player
And lived in Waco Court in Pickwick.

He had a Gibson Les Paul and a Sears amplifier,
And as he had already been playing for a few years,
Learned that high volume was essential for rock 'n roll.

My dad was very active on the scene, almost immediately,
Because most of the jam sessions took place in our basement
Since it was too much work to move the drums.

Once we added a bass player to the mix
My dad would scream at us to turn it down and then complain
About the bass causing excessive vibrations to the toilet seat upstairs.

Notwithstanding the images of my father's rumblings,
I continued progressing on my Ludwig's
And knew that I had made the right choice in buying them.

I was 'in the pink' with my drums.

Larry Levy

The Presence of Soul

One week when my parents were away gallivanting,
My grandmother stayed with us, my brother, my sister, and me,
Which meant we could do whatever we wanted.

Even our dog Rocky, usually upset and mad about something,
Was thrilled that she would wash his food bowl every day,
And let him run outside with the other aggrieved mutts.

One night after I finished my homework,
I went down to the playroom where my Ludwig drums were
And began banging out some sort of tribal beat.

When I looked up, 'Gram' was sitting on the sofa
With Rocky by her side, watching me rock and flail,
Never complaining about the noise or holding her ears.

When I finished, she told me how good it sounded.
I was confused because neither of my parents
Nor any adults ever complimented me on my playing.

She was the first grownup who got it,
Unlike my grandfather on my mom's side
Who asked me if I could play,
"Tie a Yellow Ribbon 'Round the Old Oak Tree".

My father would frequently say of his mother,
"She'd give you the shirt off her back"
To remind me about my grandmother's generosity.

But that night she gave me something even greater.

Ahoy, Landlubbers!

Landlubbers were low-riding, hip-hugging dungarees
That fit snug against the thighs and calves
Then fanned out into a giant, bell bottom.

We called them, 'Elephant Bells' due to their extreme size
And because they completely covered your shoes.
No hippie was complete without a pair of Landlubber jeans.

I wore mine every day
Along with a collared Tee and open flannel shirt.
That was the look back in 1972.

A pair of my father's black army boots
Rounded out my radical ensemble,
And like Mr. Natural, I was truckin' in style.

An unintended consequence of wearing enormous bells
Was treading on the bottom of the pant legs
Causing the jeans to tear up to the back of the knee.

My mom offered to sew the damaged area.
But unlike the fictional mother in the legendary Animals' song,
"The House of the Rising Sun" --
Who did sew her son's new blue-jeans --
I embraced my own tattered fashion statement.

Larry Levy

The Spring of My Discontent

In May of 1972 I took the bus down to Read Street,
Where, The Bum Steer, The Bead Experience,
And the rest of the Baltimore counterculture grazed,
To get my hair styled at The Hair Garage.

It was the spring of *my* discontent.
I stood in front of the mirror but behind the times.

No more Brylcreem or subservience to the god, Vitalis.
No more trying to tame wild curly hair
By combing it the opposite way.
And no more parting my hair on the side to please the parents.

I put my head in the hands
Of Chas and his bevy of creative stylists
That decided a bush was the only possible solution.

Radical change did not come easy, particularly at first.
I had to put up with ridicule from all sides.
My sister thought I looked like a tennis ball.
My parents thought I looked like Jimi Hendrix.
And some of my classmates just pointed and laughed.

But it was a new era for me.
I began to look at myself in a different light.
As my hair grew into a lion's mane
I felt the strength of Samson.

Plus, I got to carry a black Afro pick proudly in my back pocket.

Sunny's

Sunny Surplus was the anti-haberdashery
For the anti-conformist teenager looking to
Enhance his wardrobe with army-style garb.

There were several locations throughout the Baltimore area
But the store my mother took us to
Was located on Liberty Road just west of Milford Mill Road.

Sunny's was the place to go after one established their 'head'
And realized that underdressing was more important than
Dressing to impress or conforming like the 'straights.'

When you walked into the store you were immediately hit
By wooden crates full of dummy hand grenades
And garments that hung seemingly from everywhere.

I never cared much for the military fatigue-styled clothing
But the trench coat had a special place in my heart
As did the lace up black army boots.

I went mostly for the thick, flannel shirts
That I wore unbuttoned over a colored tee shirt
Every day for most of high school.

My dad who served in the army and was always quick to point out
The inconsistences and weird behavior of his son
Said, "you'll wear the clothes but won't serve."

Larry Levy

As If

It all began in the woods
That separated our house from Pikesville Senior High
When I stole some Kent cigarettes from my mom.

I quickly realized the awful taste of tobacco,
Gave up the senseless huffing and puffing,
And turned my attention toward something new.

Some of the older and more experienced teens
Told me about Shera bidis, an Indian cigarette,
That was easily had and could also get you high.
But the bugle shaped leaf tasted worse than my mom's Kent's
And failed to deliver on the promise of inebriation.

So, when marijuana became available to me
It was only natural to give it a try, despite all the risks
That went far beyond the mischievous pranks of childhood.

My father always threatened to strangle
The person who "started me on pot", as he used to say.
As if, my parents smoking to be cool and tranquilize
Had no effect on my looking to imitate.

As if, the movies they showed in 9th grade science class
Talking about the dangers of marijuana and LSD
While simultaneously hyping beautiful hippie girls
Dancing in frilly skirts to The Jefferson Airplane acted as a deterrent.

As if, eating a half-a-box of Frosted Flakes every morning,
Followed by a daily dose of Ring Dings, Pixie Stix, and Coca Cola,
Had no correlation to our wild, uncontrollable behavior.

As if!

Spirit in the Sky

I was thirteen years old when I first heard the song, "Spirit in the Sky",
And for the next two years
Was under the sway of the psychedelic masterpiece.

I never considered changing my religion,
But when a guy named Greenbaum
Sings about meeting up with Jesus
Well, it's best to pay attention.

So, I went out and bought a bronze crucifix with a leather hoop
For strictly non-religious but practical reasons:
It was a marijuana pipe in disguise.

The two ends of the T-shaped amulet unscrewed
Revealing a bowl and a screen.
The long stem running north to south
Had a long chamber with a hole
From which you drew the medicinal herb.

One day I came down into our living room
With the giant cross hanging fashionably around my neck.
My grandmother who had come over to check in on her grandchildren
Took one look at me and nearly had a coronary.

The next day my parents gave me the third degree
Forbidding me to wear the crucifix.
They wanted to know who was responsible for my conversion.

So, I blamed it on Norman Greenbaum.
My dad immediately called my Hebrew school
To root out the radical trouble maker.

Larry Levy

The irony was not lost on me
When I asked him, "what would Jesus say?"
I was grounded for a week with no one to answer my prayers.

Almost All the Way

In the wild, unsupervised summer after sophomore year,
A friend of mine and I
Would hang out at the Greenspring Shopping Center,
Meet new girls from who knows where and drive around.

One night I hit it off with this tall, lean girl
That I met in front of the bowling alley.
It was obvious that she and I were going places.

With my friend behind the wheel of his mom's
Beautiful, red, Ford Galaxy 500 convertible,
My new squeeze and I began to explore each other in the backseat.

But curious eyes appeared in the rear-view mirror
One too many times for my love interest to remain forthcoming,
So, I told my friend to pull the car over
Where she and I agreed the trunk was our best option.

We immediately began kissing and feeling for each other in the dark.
The things I wanted were exactly where I imagined them to be,
And although I was denied the pleasure of sight
My firsthand experience gave me great satisfaction.
I was having the most fun a guy could possibly have
In a space usually reserved for a spare tire, jack, and crowbar.

But our impulsive need for privacy
Was now overshadowed by an even greater desire to get out.
When my friend opened the trunk, he found us completely clothed,
Only a little dirtier than he had seen us before.

Love can rebound after many mishaps,
But sharp curves, pot holes, and exhaust fumes
Have a way of putting the kibosh on even the best laid plans.

Larry Levy

The Marriottsville Carnival

There was something special about a summer carnival
That brought out the best in teenage girls.

Even if you factored in the competition,
We were a couple of guys with a blue Chevy Impala
Which meant we could offer a ride
That was better than the ones they had to buy tickets for.

One night my friend and I met these two girls
That lived less than a mile from the firehouse
Where the Marriottsville carnival was in full swing.

We exchanged phone numbers
And an invitation to a small party the following week
At the home of the prettier girl who liked my friend.

The ride out to the party now included another guy
That lived down the street in Oakton Court
Because once the word got out, he wanted in.

But when we got to the party there were no other girls.
My friend the driver, and leader of the neighborhood,
Took off with the hostess, leaving me and the third wheel
With the girl that was supposed to be mine.

Since our ride home was getting lucky in another room,
My friend from down the street and I took one for the team.
We stayed up all night, talking, laughing,
Listening to music, and partying until we passed out.

When morning broke, the hostess informed us
That we had to split because her parents
Would be home in a few hours.

When All Was Well In Wellwood

The three of us said our farewells and got in the car,
And as luck would have it, the Impala wouldn't start.
So, we had no other choice but to hoof it.

Home was about eight miles away
So, we decided to stick out thumbs to help our cause.
A garbage truck pulled over
With three guys laughing in the front seat.

I grabbed the giant white staple on the back of the truck
While my friends hung onto the passenger's side mirror.
The truck started weaving in and out of traffic
And sped down Liberty Road at 70 mph.

The driver pulled over and dropped us off
At the corner of Liberty and Old Court
Where we picked up another ride with slightly less drama.

The next weekend,
We were right back at the Marriottsville carnival.

Mono

Sometime during the fall of 1972, the spit-swapping event took place
That inevitably resulted in my contracting mononucleosis.
It would have been difficult to finger the suspect
Because back then there was a whole-lotta-kissin'-goin'-on.

Mono, also known as, 'the kissing disease'
Was truly "the serpent underneath the flower".
If I had read *Macbeth* before eleventh grade,
And understood the reality behind the appearance of such soft lips,
I could have avoided the entire fiasco.

But instead, I was bed-ridden and out of school for eight weeks
And nearly failed out of my junior year.
The doctor said my spleen was the size of a softball.

While my sister and brother were in school, and my mom at work,
I was at home, alone, with no energy to do anything.
I hardly ate and slept for the better part of each day.

The only highlight was staring out the window
At this beautiful woman, about 10-years my senior.
She went to work and came home the same time every day.
I would fantasize about the very activity
That brought about my downfall.

Some remember their first kiss as the best.
Others consider the multitude of kisses that followed
More significant than the first.
And though my kissing career was hijacked by a debilitating virus,
I knew it was better to have kissed and lost, than
Never to have kissed at all.

The Next Level

In 1973, I got serious about the drums.
I had been playing about a year, listening to my heroes,
Teaching myself beats, and jamming with friends.

I decided it was time to move in a different direction.
So, I set my sights on the classically oriented Peabody Institute.

My mother came to my aid by enlisting her father for the funds.
Although he was somewhat of a skinflint, he ultimately obliged.
Like my father, he believed studying music was not education
And the drums were not really an instrument.

By rule, I had to audition for the preparatory with *the* drum instructor.
And though I couldn't play anything
Other than a few elementary rock beats,
I was accepted on condition I renounce my bad habits:
The way I held the sticks and my immersion in The Beatles.

So, every Friday after school,
I walked about a mile to Park Heights Avenue,
And took the #5 bus down to Mt. Vernon for an hour lesson.
On Saturdays, I returned for theory and percussion ensemble.

I learned traditional grip, read from jazz and classical books,
Played a Ludwig Musser 4-octave marimba,
And took drumming and music to the next level.

Larry Levy

Innocence is Ephemeral

It all began innocently enough
In the attic bedroom of a mutual friend
On a chilly night in Old Pikesville.

Interesting things happen when vertical, upright puppy love --
Simple-minded kid stuff from grade school –
Turns horizontal and quickly clears up your acne.

I would sleep over her house, in a separate bedroom,
Only to have her creep in during the wee hours
When her sister and parents were fast asleep.

The carnival moved to my house on Chokeberry
Where she was given my basement bedroom
And I was supposed to sleep on the purple sofa in the living room.

We had some great adventures and misadventures.
A cancelled Quicksilver Messenger Service concert
Forced us to hitchhike on Interstate I-29
From Merriweather Post Pavilion back to Pikesville.

Another time, we brought a lost dog back to her house
That became part of a family of strays,
Where everything was open and allowed.

We tried vegetarianism for awhile
And lived on a combination of Deaf Smith's Peanut Butter,
Mrs. Paul's Fish Sticks, and Tiger's Milk.

One beautiful summer day, with her older sister behind the wheel,
We drove out to Pretty Boy Dam to expand our horizons.
It was a watershed moment swimming naked in a reservoir.

When All Was Well In Wellwood

But most of our time together was spent not eating meat,
Playing with the dog, listening to music, getting high,
And talking about Socialism, peace, and love for everyone.

With senior year a month away,
She made the rash decision to drop out of high school.
Then came the pitch about moving away and getting our own place.

So, I spent the entire month of August alone,
Thinking and looking for answers in the music I loved.
I contemplated my life and our relationship.

Then, in a moment of surprising maturity,
I called her up and told her I wanted to be together,
But would not drop out of high school.

She took this as a rejection
And then turned it around and rejected me.

And there was my friend, my Wellwood compatriot,
In his mom's blue Chevy Impala, picking me up curbside
Where I sat with a letter and bag of parting gifts.

Coming back into Wellwood from neighboring Fort Garrison
Was the best therapy a depressed teenager could ask for.

Larry Levy

Watkins Glen

In the summer of 1973, between junior and senior year,
A good friend of mine heard about a concert
At the Watkin's Glen race course in upstate New York.

We were working for my uncle's construction company
And somehow got a few days off from our busy schedule
Removing the excess concrete from between the bricks
At the Sekine Brush Company building in Clipper Mill.

So, we loaded up his puke green Mercury Monterey
With two senior girls from Pikesville
And a tag-along friend that went to Milford Mill Senior High.

The road trip was fueled by tunes and pot
And the better looking of the two girls
Taking off her top to get a head start on the festivities.

We arrived at the campsite around 3am.
The two girls split as did the 'fifth wheel'.
My friend and I partied until the cockerel crowed.

The next morning around 8am
We trekked about two miles to the festival area
Where we plopped down Indian style
Around 100 yards from the main stage.

The Dead flew in by helicopter and started jamming at high noon.
They played for five hours in the scorching heat
And when they finished, so was I.

When All Was Well In Wellwood

I navigated through the hordes of people, all 600,000 of them,
And worked my way back to the car.
I started figuratively knocking on tents for food and water;
Ate a little, drank a little, and mostly got high.
My friend stayed for The Band and Allman Brothers,
And then returned to the car around 1am.

The next morning our goal was food.
We walked six miles to the local town
And bought two bags full of sandwiches, chips,
Sweets, bottles of water – whatever we could carry.

We hopped on the back of a convertible
And put the bags in the back seat.
As the car sped up the hill, I slid off the trunk
And fell onto the road, face down.

Fortunately, there were no cars behind me.
My friend jumped off and came to my aid
At which time the car took off with our groceries.

So, we scrounged for food and water,
Made friends and bartered for what we needed,
Then loaded up the car and set sail back to Baltimore.

In three days, my mind was transported to the moon and back.
I saw beautiful girls swimming naked in the lake,
And drug trucks that pedaled pot, hash, LSD, and pills.

Couples having sex out in the open
Wasn't anything like what I had experienced
With *my* girlfriend, alone, fumbling in the dark.
But I knew for certain I would never be the same.

The next day after we got home, I quit my job.

Sweet Cider

My friend and I, fresh off the road from Watkin's Glen,
Had been working on musical ideas for awhile
And began practicing in his basement on Caveswood Lane.

Sometimes we drove out to Pretty Boy Dam
Where he strummed the 6-string
And I banged and shook anything I could get my hands on.

We added a guitar player/songwriter from Milford Mill Sr.
(the late addition to our trip to Watkin's Glen),
My childhood buddy from Wellwood on bass,
And together formed Sweet Cider in 1973.

We went for a country-rock sound
And featured a mish-mosh of cover songs from Dylan,
The Beatles, The Lovin' Spoonful, Donovan,
And Creedence Clearwater Revival.

At first, we played in friends' living rooms
Or invited people over to our practice space,
But then we gradually booked bigger and better venues.

During senior year we played at Milford Mill Sr. High,
An evening gig at Pikesville Sr. in the activity room,
And to a packed crowd at Loch Raven High
For the battle of the bands.

We showcased one of our originals
At the annual junior ring ceremony
In the main auditorium at Pikesville Sr.

But it was not our creativity or playing
That got us into the class yearbook.

We would be remembered for how we appeared:
Scruffy long-hairs with fake noses and glasses
And 18" strap-on beards.

Larry Levy

"It's Aite"

My woodworking teacher at Pikesville Senior High
Wore a pair of horn-rimmed glasses and a larger than life smile.
He was my favorite of any teacher I had during those years.

He referred to me as, "Hairy", due to my giant afro.
Whenever I made a mistake in either design or execution,
He would always say, "It's Aite Hairy, it'll be okay."

The shop had a band saw, jig saw, circular saw,
As well as a joiner and my favorite, the lathe.
To say that my senior year revolved around the lathe
Would have been an understatement.

I was so enamored with carving on a lathe, that I saved up my money
And bought a brand new one from Skarie on North Howard Street.
I borrowed a drill press from my grandfather, started a pipe business,
And sold paraphernalia to the head shops around town.

My teacher gave me carte blanche when it came to making pipes
Because I also made serious stuff, like tables and drawers.
I also came up with an eight-paneled design for stash-boxes,
Using exotic woods like bubinga and purpleheart.
He even helped me cut the exact angles for each of the 16-sides.

One day while I was in the finishing room lacquering a table,
Two students were having a duel
With 90-degree angled metal t- squares.
When the teacher caught wind of what was happening,
His face turned beet red and he screamed,
"Hey, don't worry, those are only accurate measuring devices."

The students put the weapons back in their proper place.
I, along with others, roared with laughter.
It was the coolest way to reason with stupid kids doing stupid things.

Larry Levy

My Awakening

My literary greed began in senior year
When my English teacher, the coolest of the cool,
Had us read, *Siddhartha*, by Hermann Hesse.

The only other book I had read from cover to cover
Was *Call of the Wild* by Jack London in seventh grade,
But that reading failed to change my life.

In junior high I was still a child and part of a system
Where numbers, facts, dates, and memorizations
Allowed me to pass from grade to grade.

I played baseball, ran around in the neighborhood,
Hung out with friends, watched television,
Laughed and carried on without a care or much thought.

Then *Siddhartha* came along and opened my mind.
I began to see life as something more;
A journey where thinking would lead the way.

Now everything was about learning.
My first taste of love and sex turned sour,
And reading, writing, and contemplation brought sweetness.

My eyes turned inward without chemicals,
And I leaned on the insights and metaphors of others
From the books I read in the wake of *Siddhartha*.

At seventeen I was reborn.

The Last Day

First days are exciting because they are new
And hold the promise of even better days to come.

But last days bring closure
And upon reflection hopefully inspire gratitude.

Of course, such profound insights require wisdom
Which is rarely achieved by the end of high school.

It was on a June day in 1974,
The last day of my senior year and high school career,
That three friends and I decided to cut school
And drive down to Washington Music in Wheaton, Maryland.

Sure, it was always fun looking at musical equipment
You couldn't afford and didn't need,
And then eating "burgers by the bag" at Little Tavern.

But the thrill of rebelling and making a statement
On the final day of what had been a 12-year run,
Put me in an existential funk for the entire ride home.

I knew intuitively that my rebellious act was futile,
Because on this one special day
It would have been more fun being at school than not.

And if there was one thing that bothered me more than anything else
It was the thought of missing out on something
That was never to be again.

Larry Levy

After all, cutting school had been the cornerstone of my senior year
So, there was nothing new or exciting about the act itself.
What I failed to learn from first days to last
Was that if you do something too much it's not special anymore.

Epilogue

Larry Levy

You Can Never Go Home

I had been working as a computer programmer
For a couple of years when I had an "Aha!" moment:
"There has to be more to life than being anchored to a 9-5 job".

I reached into my bag of tricks
And pulled out the one about reliving a childhood fantasy
To replace the reality, I now found myself burdened with.

Baseball had been, "very, very good to me"
Through my childhood and adolescent years.
So, why not go back to a life of fun.

At the time, my father's pharmacy
Serviced the Baltimore Orioles with medicine and supplies,
Which meant he had the connections to get me a tryout with the team.

I went back to the old neighborhood, back to Wellwood,
Recruited my next-door neighbor and his catcher's mitt,
And began pitching every day
From the mound at Pikesville Senior High:
The same mound I threw from eight years before.

On the day of my tryout at Memorial Stadium,
I was escorted into the locker room
Where I donned #26, the uniform of Don Stanhouse,
And had my arm liberated by trainer Ralph Salvon.

My father and his best friend sat in the stands
While I threw strike after strike to Cal Ripken Sr.
From the Oriole bullpen, as Ray Miller, the pitching coach, looked on.

When All Was Well In Wellwood

After they had seen enough, I waved to my dad,
And went back into the locker room
Where the team was getting ready for practice.

Ray Miller and Ralph Salvon pulled me aside
And told me they liked what they saw,
Then offered me a position in the D-league in North Carolina.

I thanked them for an unforgettable experience,
And the generous offer to potentially become an Oriole someday.
My catcher-in-waiting took pictures of all the action
And Ralph Salvon tossed me the ball I used as I left the locker room.

My dad put his arm around me, told me how proud he was,
And in that unique father and son moment,
The eight years of tension between us, vanished.

I returned to work and talked about my experience, the players,
And how cool it was to be in the bullpen, on the field,
Pitching to Cal Ripken Sr. with Ray Miller taking notes.

I had already made my decision.
I knew in my heart that going back to someone I used to be
Was an escape, a way out of something I didn't like now.

So, I stayed on at work, an honest way forward,
As I had courageously done at age fifteen
When I stopped playing baseball to follow *my* dreams.

I was humbled and reminded of the words
Justin Hayward and The Moody Blues sang to me
In my basement bedroom on Chokeberry Road
When I was becoming the person, I wanted to be.

"Memories can never take you back, home, sweet home,
You can never go home anymore."